Snap
books

Designer
Dogs

Chiweenie

A Cross between a Chihuahua and a Dachshund

by Molly Kolpin

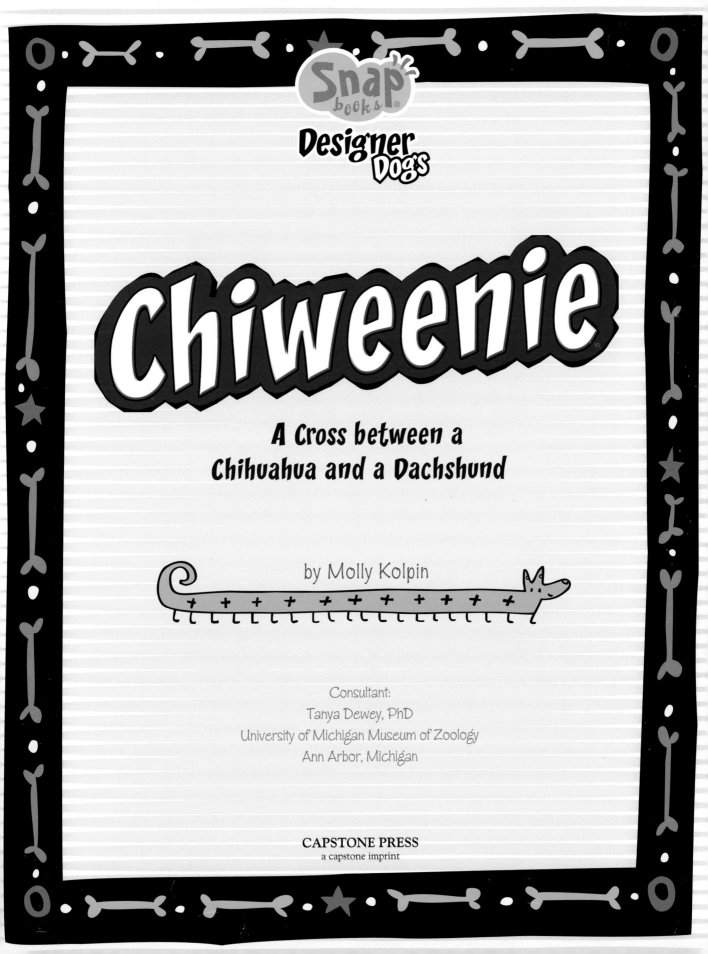

Consultant:
Tanya Dewey, PhD
University of Michigan Museum of Zoology
Ann Arbor, Michigan

CAPSTONE PRESS
a capstone imprint

Snap Books are published by Capstone Press,
1710 Roe Crest Drive, North Mankato, Minnesota 56003.
www.capstonepub.com

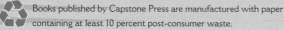

Books published by Capstone Press are manufactured with paper
containing at least 10 percent post-consumer waste.

Library of Congress Cataloging-in-Publication Data
Kolpin, Molly.
  Chiweenie : a cross between a Chihuahua and a Dachshund / by Molly Kolpin.
    p. cm.— (Snap. Designer dogs)
  Includes bibliographical references and index.
  Summary: "Describes Chiweenies, their characteristics and behavior, and includes basic information on feeding, grooming,
training, and health care"—Provided by publisher.
  ISBN 978-1-4296-7667-0 (library binding)
  1. Chiweenie—Juvenile literature.. I. Title.
  SF429.C49K65 2012
  636.76—dc23   2011036705

Editorial Credits
Editor: Lori Shores
Designer: Veronica Correia
Media Researcher: Marcie Spence
Photo Stylist: Sarah Schuette
Studio Scheduler: Marcy Morin
Production Specialist: Kathy McColley

Photo Credits
123RF: Kelly Richardson, 18, 29; Capstone Studio: Karon Dubke, cover (top), 4, 6, 7, 11, 15, 16, 17, 19, 20, 21, 22, 23, 24, 25, 27, 28;
iStockphoto: DeborahMaxemow, 8; Shutterstock: Andrey Bandurenko, 13 (bottom), Eric Isselee, cover (bottom right), Gertjan
Hooijer, 12, Pospisil MRL, 10, Utekhina Anna, cover (bottom left), 9, Wallenrock, 13 (top); Superstock Inc.: Damon Craig, 5

Printed in the United States of America in North Mankato, Minnesota.
102011   006405CGS12

Table of Contents

Chapter 1

Teeny Chiweenies

Chiweenies may have little bodies, but don't be fooled. These small dogs have big hearts and big attitudes. They're outgoing and social but seem to enjoy being at home with family best. They're loyal dogs, so they can sometimes be protective of their families. They will often yap at anything that crosses paths with their owners.

Although Chiweenies try to appear tough, they make loving pets. Chiweenies are known for being friendly. Chiweenie owners say these little dogs are easygoing and playful. These **traits** have made the Chiweenie a popular designer dog.

trait—a quality or characteristic that makes one person or animal different from another

WHAT ARE DESIGNER DOGS?

Morkies are a mix of Maltese and Yorkshire Terrier dogs.

A designer dog is a mix of two **purebred** dogs. Designer dogs aren't purebreds themselves, but they're not mutts, either. Mutts are unplanned combinations of different **breeds**. Designer dogs are purposely bred. They're also called crossbreeds.

The Labradoodle was one of the first designer dogs. In the 1980s, breeder Wally Conron needed a guide dog that wouldn't affect someone with allergies. He knew Labrador Retrievers made excellent guide dogs. And Poodles are less likely to cause allergic reactions than other breeds. By mixing the two dogs, he created puppies that shared traits from both parents.

Soon people realized they could combine breeds for other purposes too. Some people breed dogs that shed very little. Others create crossbreeds that will do well in dog sports or contests. Some designer dogs are bred just to be good family pets.

purebred—having parents of the same breed

breed—a certain kind of animal within an animal group; breed also means to mate and raise a certain kind of animal

Labradoodle

Join the Club!

The American Kennel Club (AKC) doesn't recognize designer dogs as true breeds. The AKC sets standards for the appearance and behavior of purebred dogs. But designer dogs do not always look and behave the same way. The American Canine Hybrid Club (ACHC) is a club for crossbreed dogs. Breeders can register designer dogs with this organization.

Chapter 2

Behind the Breed

Chiweenie

Learning about parent breeds will help you understand a crossbreed dog better. After all, puppies will look and behave like their parents. In the Chiweenie's case, the parent breeds are the Dachshund and the Chihuahua.

DACHSHUNDS

Dachshunds originally came from Germany where they were used for hunting badgers. In fact, their name means "badger dog" in German. Their long, thin bodies were perfect for getting into underground badger dens. And their strong fighting skills made them tough matches for fierce badgers. Today most Dachshunds are kept as pets, but they still show signs of their hunting history. These feisty, energetic dogs can often be found burrowing in the dirt or tunneling under bedcovers.

Dachshund

Dog Fact!

Dachshunds are sometimes called "wiener dogs." This nickname makes up the second part of the Chiweenie's name.

With their unique bodies, Dachshunds are easy to recognize. But while all Dachshunds have long backs and short legs, their coats can be different. Common coat colors include red, cream, black, and brown. Their fur can be short and smooth, wirehaired, or longhaired.

Of course, Dachshunds aren't right for everyone. They're intelligent dogs, but can be stubborn. Dachshunds require much time and patience for training. But those willing to put in the extra effort are often rewarded with a wonderful pet.

CHIHUAHUAS

Chihuahuas are the smallest of all dog breeds. They have large, pointy ears that stick straight up. Their coats can be almost any color. Some have long fur, while others have short, smooth fur. Because their little bodies are fragile, they can be easily injured. They aren't good choices for families with young children who may play too rough. And like Dachshunds, Chihuahuas can be difficult to train. But these little dogs can be wonderful pets for the right people. Chihuahuas are best for people who can patiently care for and train them.

Chihuahua

Despite their small size, Chihuahuas have big voices and bold attitudes. They are always on alert and welcome visitors with a bark. Because they're fiercely devoted to their owners, Chihuahuas can be aggressive with strangers. Special care should be taken to **socialize** these dogs at a young age to avoid problems. At home, however, Chihuahuas are sweet pets that enjoy cuddling. This trait may come from their history as lap dogs for Mexico's upper class.

socialize—to train to get along with people and other dogs

Dachshund puppies

Beware of Puppy Mills!

Dachshunds and Chihuahuas are popular dogs, but some people take advantage of that. Some breeders are more interested in profit than in proper care of animals. These breeders raise as many puppies as possible. The dogs are kept in terrible conditions and often develop health problems. Always be sure to meet the breeder and see the conditions in which the puppies are raised.

Chapter 3

A Winning Combination

Chiweenies were bred mainly for medical reasons. Breeders wanted a dog with the personality of the Dachshund. They also wanted to avoid the back problems Dachshunds often develop. They hoped they could create a healthier breed by mixing Dachshunds with Chihuahuas. However, many Chiweenies still suffer from back problems. But as pets, these merry little dogs are a great success.

Chiweenies look like a combination of their parents. Most have large, batlike Chihuahua ears. They usually have the Chihuahua's big, expressive eyes too. But Chiweenies get their long, low backs from the Dachshund.

Coat colors differ greatly among Chiweenies. Common colors are brown, black, and tan. Coat types also vary. Depending on the parents, a Chiweenie can have short or medium-length fur.

SMALL DOGS BIG PERSONALITIES

The Chiweenie's most common trait is its small size. Even as adults, Chiweenies weigh only 5 to 10 pounds (2.3 to 4.5 kilograms). They stand just 8 inches (20 centimeters) tall on their tiny legs. Chiweenies are playful and brave, but they're too small to handle rough play or fighting. Their long, injury-prone backs make them especially fragile.

Although small, Chiweenies have very big personalities. These tiny dogs sometimes start fights with animals many times their size. And despite their little legs, Chiweenies can run at surprisingly fast speeds. These dogs love chasing small animals. Their love for activity and adventure comes largely from their Dachshund parents.

Dog Fact!

Some people think dogs with differently colored eyes are unlucky. Not true! It's rare for dogs to have mismatched eyes, but it can happen in any breed.

From the Chihuahua's history as a loyal lap dog, Chiweenies have a protective nature. They keep close watch over their owners and make devoted companions. Owners protect their fragile Chiweenies, but most Chiweenies believe they must protect their owners. A Chiweenie is likely to consider itself an important member of the family. And many owners agree that their Chiweenies are indeed much more than pets.

But Chiweenies aren't all bark. They are curious and friendly. Chiweenies that are socialized when young can get along well with children and other pets. Without proper socialization, Chiweenies may bark angrily at strangers and be aggressive toward other animals.

Many Dogs to Choose From

Though Chiweenies make loving pets, they aren't the best choice for everyone. Consider visiting an animal shelter to meet dogs of all kinds. Animal shelters are full of animals that need a good home. And whether purebred, designer dog, or mutt, the dog's personality is always what matters most.

Chapter 4

Chiweenie Care

Owning a dog comes with many rewards. But it also comes with many responsibilities. Without proper care, Chiweenies can become unhealthy and difficult to manage. Keep your Chiweenie happy and healthy by giving it the proper love, training, and attention.

TRAINING

All dogs need to be trained. Since Chiweenies can be stubborn, training is especially important. Be prepared to **housebreak** a Chiweenie right away. Many owners say housebreaking a Chiweenie can be a long and frustrating task. But if you are consistent, your pet will learn the right thing to do.

Obedience training is also important for Chiweenies and other dogs. Begin by teaching basic commands such as sit, stay, and come. These commands will help keep your pet safe and under control in most situations. Use repetition and praise to make training sessions successful. And be sure to train your Chiweenie not to jump off furniture or hop up steps. These actions could seriously injure its long back.

housebreak—to teach a dog where to pee and poop

obedience training—teaching an animal to obey commands

FEEDING

Responsible dog owners feed their pets at regular times each day. Purchase food made for small breeds and follow the feeding instructions on the package. Make sure your Chiweenie doesn't overeat. As with Dachshunds, any extra weight puts stress on a Chiweenie's long back. Keep human foods well out of reach so your Chiweenie doesn't eat beyond its needs.

EXERCISE

Owners can control their Chiweenie's weight by providing daily exercise. Because Chiweenies are small, they usually have enough room to run and play in a small fenced yard or apartment. But for such small dogs, Chiweenies have high energy levels. Playing a game of fetch or chase will provide good exercise for your dog. It's also a wonderful way to bond with your pet.

Chiweenies will also welcome a daily walk. Walking helps your dog get exercise and prevents it from becoming bored. Chiweenies are intelligent dogs that can get restless if left alone all day. They will likely get into trouble if they don't have something to keep them occupied. A short walk each day will provide fun exploring time for your Chiweenie.

VISITING THE VET

All dogs need regular medical checkups. Veterinarians check for health problems and give **vaccinations**. If your dog is ill, veterinarians can also give medicine or perform operations.

When taking your Chiweenie for a checkup, be sure the veterinarian examines your dog's back. Some Chiweenies suffer from a back disease. This disease can cause serious injury and pain to your Chiweenie.

vaccination—a shot of medicine that protects animals from a disease

GROOMING

Chiweenies require little grooming compared to most dogs. Chiweenies with short, thin fur only need brushing once a week. Even Chiweenies with longer fur can get by with just a weekly brushing. During grooming sessions, pay close attention to their eyes, ears, and feet. Their nails need trimming once a month. Have an adult clip their nails with a clipper made for dogs.

Give your Chiweenie a bath only when it gets dirty. Try not to bathe it more than once a month. Bathing too often may dry out your Chiweenie's skin, causing flaking and itching. Use dog shampoo for your Chiweenie, which is gentler than shampoo made for humans.

Brushing Teeth

Small dogs can have more problems with their teeth than larger dogs. Chiweenies should have their teeth brushed every day. A veterinarian can show you how to brush your dog's teeth. Use a toothbrush and toothpaste made for dogs. Don't expect that it will smell minty fresh! Dog toothpaste is often meat-flavored.

Chapter 5

Adopting a Chiweenie

Once you decide which traits would best fit in your family, it's time to find your pet. For this, you'll need to visit an animal shelter or trusted breeder. Even though Chiweenies are popular pets, they may still end up in shelters. If there aren't any Chiweenies at your local shelter, look online for other shelters nearby.

ANSWER THE FOLLOWING QUESTIONS HONESTLY. IF YOU RESPOND YES TO MOST QUESTIONS, A CHIWEENIE MAY BE A GOOD FIT FOR YOUR FAMILY.

1. Does your family have the time to properly care for a Chiweenie?

2. Are you willing to take your dog on a daily walk?

3. Can you remain patient and positive while training a dog?

4. Do you have a safe area where your dog can run and play?

5. Are you prepared to deal with the potential back problems of this dog?

CHOOSING A CHIWEENIE

If you visit a breeder, there may be more than one Chiweenie to choose from. If so, watch the dogs carefully to determine their **temperaments**. Don't just look for the dog you think is cutest. After all, a cute dog may not have a cute personality. Just take your time, and eventually you'll find the right Chiweenie for your family.

temperament—the combination of an animal's behavior and personality

LIVING WITH YOUR FOUR-LEGGED FRIEND

Don't expect your new pal to behave perfectly right away. You may even have moments of frustration as you begin training your Chiweenie. But keep in mind that dog ownership is a two-way street. Love and care for your Chiweenie, and you'll find your Chiweenie will love and care for you in return.

Glossary

breed (BREED)—a certain kind of animal within an animal group; breed also means to mate and raise a certain kind of animal

housebreak (HOUSS-brayk)—to teach a dog where to pee and poop

obedience training (oh-BEE-dee-uhns TRAY-ning)—teaching an animal to obey commands

purebred (PYOOR-bred)—having parents of the same breed

socialize (SOH-shuh-lize)—to train to get along with people and other dogs

temperament (TEM-pur-uh-muhnt)—the combination of an animal's behavior and personality

trait (TRATE)—a quality or characteristic that makes one person or animal different from another

vaccination (vak-suh-NAY-shun)—a shot of medicine that protects animals from a disease

Read More

Gagne, Tammy. *Chihuahuas.* All about Dogs. Mankato, Minn.: Capstone Press, 2009.

Lunis, Natalie. *Dachshund: The Hot Dogger.* Little Dogs Rock! New York: Bearport Pub., 2009.

Niven, Felicia Lowenstein. *Learning to Care for a Dog.* Beginning Pet Care with American Humane. Berkeley Heights, N.J.: Bailey Books/Enslow, 2011.

Internet Sites

FactHound offers a safe, fun way to find Internet sites related to this book. All of the sites on FactHound have been researched by our staff.

Here's all you do:

Visit *www.facthound.com*

Type in this code: 9781429676670

Index